WORLD WAR I

Remembering
the Great War

THE END OF WORLD WAR I

The Treaty of Versailles and Its Tragic Legacy

ALAN SWAYZE

 Crabtree Publishing Company

www.crabtreebooks.com

WORLD WAR I

Remembering the Great War

Author: Alan Swayze
Editor: Lynn Peppas
Proofreader: Lisa Slone, Wendy Scavuzzo
Editorial director: Kathy Middleton
Production coordinator: Shivi Sharma
Design Concept: Margaret Amy Salter
Cover design: Ken Wright
Photo research: Nivisha Sinha,
    Crystal Sikkens
Maps: Contentra Technologies
Print coordinator: Katherine Berti

Written, developed, and produced by
    Contentra Technologies

Cover: The heads of state at the signing
    of peace in the Hall of Mirrors,
    Versailles, June 28, 1919
Title Page: British Prime Minister
    Lloyd George, French Premier
    Georges Clemenceau, and U.S.
    President Woodrow Wilson in
    Paris during negotiations for
    the Treaty of Versailles
Contents Page: German troops in the
    streets of Soissons following the
    capture of the town on May 29, 1918

Photo Credits:
Alamy: 11 (© akg-images), 27 (© Trinity Mirror/Mirrorpix)
The Bridgeman Art Library: 21 (Shooting down a Zeppelin during the First World
    War, Hardy, Wilf (Wilfred) (20th century)/Private Collection/© Look and Learn),
    22 (The sinking of the Llandovery Castle (gouache on paper), English School, (20th
    century)/Private Collection/© Look and Learn), 23 (The British Dreadnought
    Warspite (colour litho), Davis, George Horace (1881-1960) (after) / Private
    Collection/© Look and Learn), 37 (Germany is crushed by the Treaty of Versailles,
    1931 (colour litho), Schilling, E. (fl.1923)/Private Collection/Archives Charmet)
Corbis: 15, 25b (© Bettmann), 29 (© Bettmann), 34 (Universal Images Group),
    35l (© Hulton-Deutsch Collection), 38 (© The Print Collector), 39 (© Bettmann), 40
    (© Bettmann), 42 (© Stapleton Collection), 44 (© Walter Bibikow/JAI)
Getty Images: 9 (Print Collector/Getty Images), 10 (Mondadori via Getty Images), 25t
    (Hulton Archive), 28 (Heritage Images), 34 (Universal Images Group),
© Imperial War Museums (Q 87926): Content Page
Library of Congress: 4 (LC-DIG-ggbain-15555), 14 (LC-USZ62-13028),
    16 (LC-DIG-ppmsca-04928), 17 (LC-USZ62-124516), 18 (LC-USZ62-49029),
    24 (LC-USZC4-11358), 30 (LC-USZC4-11161), 31 (LC-DIG-ggbain-13711),
    35r (LC-DIG-hec-20948),
Royal Collection: 32 (George V in coronation robes)
Shutterstock.com: 18t (Olemac)
U.S. Signal Corps photo: 12 (Edward N. Jackson)
U.S. National Archives and Records Administration: 33
Wikipedia Commons: 19 (Wilfred Owen plate from Poems (1920))
Cover: Wikimedia Commons: Imperial War Museum Collections
Title: © Bettmann/CORBIS
Back cover: Wikimedia Commons: Library and Archives Canada (background)
    Shutterstock: I. Pilon (medals); Shuttertock: IanC66 (airplane)

t=Top, b=Bottom, l=Left, r=Right

Library and Archives Canada Cataloguing in Publication

Swayze, Alan, 1951-, author
    The end of World War I : the Treaty of Versailles and its tragic legacy /
Alan Swayze.

(World War I : remembering the Great War)
Includes index.
Issued in print and electronic formats.
ISBN 978-0-7787-0388-4 (bound).--ISBN 978-0-7787-0394-5 (pbk.).--
ISBN 978-1-4271-7506-9 (pdf).--ISBN 978-1-4271-7500-7 (html)

    1. Paris Peace Conference (1919-1920)--Juvenile literature. 2. Treaty
of Versailles (1919 June 28)--Juvenile literature. 3. World War, 1914-1918--
Peace--Juvenile literature. 4. World War, 1914-1918--Influence--Juvenile
literature. I. Title.

D644.S83 2014   j940.3'141   C2014-903262-5
                                           C2014-903263-3

Library of Congress Cataloging-in-Publication Data

Swayze, Alan.
  The End of World War I : the Treaty of Versailles and its tragic legacy /
Alan Swayze.
      pages cm. -- (World War I: remembering the Great War)
  Includes index.
  ISBN 978-0-7787-0388-4 (reinforced library binding : alk. paper) -- ISBN
978-0-7787-0394-5 (pbk. : alk. paper) -- ISBN 978-1-4271-7506-9 (electronic
pdf : alk. paper) -- ISBN 978-1-4271-7500-7 (electronic html : alk. paper)
  1. World War, 1914-1918--Peace--Juvenile literature. 2. Treaty of Versailles (1919)--Juvenile literature. 3. Paris Peace Conference (1919-1920)--
Juvenile literature. 4. World War, 1914-1918--Influence--Juvenile
literature. I. Title. II. Title: End of World War One.

D644.S93 2014
940.3'141--dc23
                                           2014017860

Crabtree Publishing Company

www.crabtreebooks.com   1-800-387-7650

Printed in Canada/052014/MA20140505

Published in Canada
Crabtree Publishing
616 Welland Ave.
St. Catharines, Ontario
L2M 5V6

Published in the United States
Crabtree Publishing
PMB 59051
350 Fifth Avenue, 59th Floor
New York, New York 10118

Published in the United Kingdom
Crabtree Publishing
Maritime House
Basin Road North, Hove
BN41 1WR

Published in Australia
Crabtree Publishing
3 Charles Street
Coburg North
VIC, 3058

CONTENTS

FROM WAR TO TROUBLED PEACE

World War I was a global war centered in Europe, beginning in July 1914. By the time the war ended in November 1918, more than 10 million **combatants** lost their lives. Four empires ceased to exist. The political map of the world had changed dramatically. The events of World War I had a significant impact on the 20th century.

BELOW: *Archduke Franz Ferdinand, his wife Sophie, and their children*

THE WAR BEGINS

The war began with the assassination of Archduke Franz Ferdinand by a Bosnian-Serb on June 28, 1914. The archduke was heir to the throne of the Austro-Hungarian Empire.

In response, Austria-Hungary delivered an **ultimatum** to Serbia. International **alliances** came into effect. On July 28, 1914, Austria-Hungary attacked Serbia. Russia, Serbia's ally, **mobilized** its army in response. The alliances soon drew Germany and France into the conflict as well.

Germany invaded **neutral** Belgium and Luxembourg, while moving toward France. The invasion of Belgium led Britain to declare war on Germany. The major powers would split into two sides. Britain, France, and Russia would form the Allies. Germany and Austria-Hungary would form the Central Powers. The conflict that would become known as World War I quickly spread around the globe.

THE WAR ENDS

Although the war started quickly, it was soon bogged down in the **stalemate** of trench warfare. The Central Powers seemed to sweep ahead in the early months. However, three years of horrific fighting took their toll. In late 1917, Russia withdrew from the war.

Germany hoped to send soldiers from the Eastern Front to fight on the Western Front. However, it needed troops to secure the territories it gained in the treaty with Russia.

In 1918, Germany staged a major offensive along the Western Front. However, the Allies drove the German troops back in a series of successful **counterattacks**. At the same time, American forces entered the war on the Allied side. Germany agreed to an **armistice** on November 11, 1918. World War I ended in a victory for the Allies.

A BITTER DEFEAT

After the war, the map of Europe was redrawn. The German and Russian Empires were forced to free certain states they had controlled before the war. The Austro-Hungarian and Ottoman Empires were dissolved. Their **annexed** territories were divided among the victors.

The League of Nations was formed to prevent such a conflict from happening again. However, the organization failed. Europe was left with weakened states, economic crises, and renewed **nationalism**. Germany felt humiliated by its loss. The harsh punishment forced on Germany under the Treaty of Versailles created resentment. This resentment would give rise to **fascism** and another world war.

European Powers Before World War I

Legend:
- Allied (Entente) Powers
- Central Powers
- Neutral Powers
- Neutral Countries that joined Central Powers Later
- Neutral Countries that joined Allied Powers Later
- * Italy was aligned with Germany in 1914 but joined the war on the Allied side in 1915

EUROPEAN POWERS BEFORE WORLD WAR I

As shown in the map above, the Central Powers included three empires: the German Empire, the Austro-Hungarian Empire, and the Ottoman Empire. Bulgaria also belonged to the Central Powers. Allied Powers included Great Britain, France, the Russian Empire, Portugal, Romania, Serbia, and Greece.

European Powers After World War I

Norway
Sweden
Estonia
Denmark
BALTIC SEA
Latvia
Lithuania
NORTH SEA
East Prussia
Great Britain
Netherlands
Germany
Poland
U.S.S.R
Belgium
Luxembourg
Czechoslovakia
ATLANTIC OCEAN
France
Switzerland
Austria
Hungary
Romania
Yugoslavia
Italy
Bulgaria
Portugal
Spain
Albania
Greece
Turkey
Africa
MEDITERRANEAN SEA

EUROPEAN POWERS AFTER WORLD WAR I

The map of Europe after the war was quite different than it was before the war. The four empires were gone. The U.S.S.R., or United Soviet Socialist Republic, replaced the Russian Empire. The creation of the U.S.S.R. combined all the countries ruled by the former Russian Empire into one large country, under one government and one flag. While Great Britain and France remained the same, Germany was much smaller.

CHAPTER 1

THE END OF WORLD WAR I

World War I did not end all at once. Different treaties were made between the different nations involved. In fact, the first treaty between Russia and the Central Powers was signed while fighting continued. Serious trouble at home had forced Russia to surrender. A revolution was growing against **Czar** Nicholas II. When the revolutionaries won, they decided to pull Russia out of the war.

> **WHAT DO YOU THINK?**
> How did the Bolsheviks affect Russia's role in the war?

> [The Germans' efforts to reintroduce Lenin to Russia were done] "in the same way that you might send a phial [a small glass container] containing a **culture** of **typhoid** or of **cholera** to be poured into the water supply of a great city."
>
> WINSTON CHURCHILL
> (LATER TO BE BRITISH PRIME MINISTER)

RUSSIA'S WITHDRAWAL FROM THE WAR

Before the war, Russian revolutionary Vladimir Lenin had been jailed then **exiled** for his attempts to overthrow the Russian government. Lenin was against Russia's involvement in the war. He believed that the workers and lower classes were being used in this conflict by their rulers. He led a group called the Bolsheviks. He called on the Russian people to overthrow the czar and others responsible for sending them to war to be killed. The Germans helped revolutionaries such as Lenin. They hoped Lenin would cause problems between the Russian people and their government.

Revolution in Russia

Russian citizens were suffering in their daily lives. They lacked many basic necessities such as food. People began to riot and go on strike throughout the country. During the February Revolution of 1917, Russian army troops sympathized with the strikers and joined them. The czar fired his government. But they secretly formed a provisional, or temporary, government to replace the czar. The czar was forced to **abdicate**.

The provisional government continued the war against the Central Powers, against the people's wishes.

Weighing the situation in Russia, the Germans allowed Lenin to travel secretly through Germany from Switzerland to Russia. Once back in Russia, Lenin worked to overthrow the unpopular provisional government. He rallied the people with his call for "peace, land, and bread." Between November 6 and 8, the Bolshevik-led Red Guards overthrew the provisional government. They declared Russia to be the world's first **Marxist** state. Lenin was its leader.

His new government immediately took steps to make peace with Germany. Within weeks, fighting between the Germans and Russians on the Eastern Front ended. A peace conference began at Brest-Litovsk, in what is now the city of Brest in Belarus, on December 22, 1917.

Treaty of Brest-Litovsk

The negotiations for the Treaty of Brest-Litovsk lasted for several months. Delegates had to find terms that both parties could agree on. On March 3, 1918, Russian and German representatives signed the treaty. Russia lost control of the **Baltic States**, Poland, and Finland, and gave up other provinces and districts. Ukraine became an independent state under German military occupation. As a result of the surrender, Russia lost more than 350,000 square miles (906,496 sq km) and 50 million people living in those areas.

The Treaty of Brest-Litovsk

Limit of German-occupied area under treaty

German advance at time of armistice

Land occupied by Central Powers after treaty

0   200 Miles
0   200 Kms

Sweden

Finland

St. Petersburg (Petrograd)

BALTIC SEA

Estonia

Livonia

Russia

Moscow

Lithuania

Germany

Warsaw

Poland

Ukraine

Rostov

Austria-Hungary

Belgrade   Romania
       Bucharest
Serbia   Bulgaria   BLACK SEA

BELOW: *Lenin addressing a 1917 meeting of Soviets*

Results of the Treaty

Under Brest-Litovsk, Russia ceased to be one of the Allies. Germany annexed the lands it had been seeking in the East.

However, the treaty caused problems for Germany. German troops were needed to occupy new territory. Bolshevik ideas encouraging revolution began to spread as well. These issues started in Austria and soon moved to Germany. The war also disrupted agriculture in the occupied areas. This created food shortages for soldiers and at home. Finally, long debates over the terms of the Treaty of Brest-Litovsk delayed moving German soldiers in the East to the Western Front where they were badly needed. Indeed, the German victory was costly.

THE UNITED STATES AND THE END OF THE WAR

Certain key events, such as the sinking of the *Lusitania* and German unrestricted submarine warfare (on pages 22–23), drew the United States into the war. On April 2, 1917, President Woodrow Wilson addressed a joint session of Congress. He told them that neutrality was no longer an option. The United States declared war four days later.

The Fourteen Points

President Wilson addressed another joint session of Congress on January 8, 1918,

ABOVE: *Diplomats and military officers from Russia and the Central Powers met to sign the Treaty of Brest-Litovsk.*

to assure Americans that they were fighting for a moral cause and for peace in Europe. "The Fourteen Points" outlined in this speech would later become the basis for the terms of the German surrender.

Germany Fights On

Even with the United States joining the Allies, German expectations remained high. German leaders launched the Operation Michael offensive in March 1918. They were not able to keep it up, however. A French counterattack in July erased German gains. With more and more American troops arriving in Europe, a victory for the Central Powers began to look unlikely.

The Armistice Is Signed

When the guns finally fell silent on November 11, 1918, Germans looked forward to peace. The German government had asked President Wilson to help set up the general armistice.

They wanted the Fourteen Points to form the groundwork for a fair and lasting peace. At 5:00 a.m. that day, an armistice with Germany was signed in a railroad carriage at Compiègne, France. The **ceasefire** was to go into effect at 11 a.m. on November 11—"the eleventh hour of the eleventh day of the eleventh month." Leading up to the time when the treaty would go into effect, armies on both sides withdrew from their defensive positions.

However, some fighting continued on other fronts as commanders wanted to capture territory before the war ended. Immediately following the armistice, American, Belgian, British, and French forces occupied the Rhineland in western Germany.

Blockade on Germany Maintained

The Allies continued their naval **blockade** of Germany for eight months after the armistice was signed. Food shortages in Germany had already pushed many civilians to starvation. Continuing the blockade caused hundreds of thousands more deaths, as many German civilians starved. This produced in many Germans a sense of despair and anger toward the victors.

RIGHT: *Formal signing of the armistice, November 11, 1918*

Paris Peace Conference of 1919

The peace conference that led to the Treaty of Versailles began in Paris in January 1919. No leaders from Germany or Russia were invited. The major world leaders attending included French Premier Georges Clemenceau, British Prime Minister David Lloyd George, Italian Prime Minister Vittorio Orlando, and U.S. President Woodrow Wilson. Wilson soon found that Clemenceau and Lloyd George **dominated** the conference and that they showed little interest in his Fourteen Points. Both leaders had been facing angry voters at home. People were demanding harsh punishment for the losing side.

THE TREATY OF VERSAILLES

The Treaty of Versailles was signed on June 28, 1919. It officially ended the state of war between the Allies and Germany. Other Central Power nations signed separate treaties with the Allies.

The British Naval Blockade of Germany

Northern patrol and mines

Naval war zone declared by Germany in 1915

Dover patrol and mines

RIGHT: *Attending the Paris Peace Conference (left to right): David Lloyd George from Britain, Vittorio Orlando from Italy, Georges Clemenceau from France, and U. S. President Woodrow Wilson*

Terms of the Treaty

The French and British wanted Germany to be punished harshly. They ignored Wilson's Fourteen Points for the treaty because they didn't believe them to be harsh enough.

Territorial Losses Germany lost its colonies and a large part of its own territory in the treaty: West Prussia, part of East Prussia, Schleswig, Upper Silesia, Danzig, and Memel. Alsace-Lorraine was also returned to France. The new League of Nations, established as part of the treaty, assumed control of the Saar region, and the entire Rhineland was to be occupied for up to 15 years. The treaty also said that Germany could not unite with Austria.

The territorial losses cut the total German population by 10 percent. The losses humiliated Germany.

Military Restrictions The German army could be no larger than 100,000 men. Naval forces were limited to 15,000 men and 6 battleships, with only 36 ships total. Military weapons specifically outlawed included aircraft, submarines, and tanks.

War Guilt Clause, Article 231 Under Article 231, Germany was forced to admit guilt for starting the war and required to pay heavy penalties. Germans later would call this the War Guilt Clause. German war debt came to 266 gold marks, equal to roughly 63 billion U.S. dollars at the time.

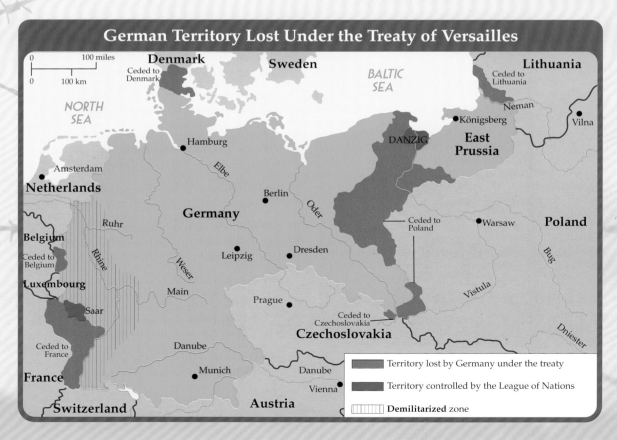

German Territory Lost Under the Treaty of Versailles

☐	Territory lost by Germany under the treaty
☐	Territory controlled by the League of Nations
⦚⦚⦚	Demilitarized zone

The German officials were stunned and outraged when they heard the terms. In fact, leading experts of the time protested that Germany's paying out such a huge amount could damage the global economy. France and Britain insisted on the payments anyway. The treaty included clauses stating that Germany could be punished further if it failed to pay on time. Although the Germans felt betrayed, their backs were up against a wall. They were forced to sign or risk greater punishments.

The League of Nations The treaty included one of Wilson's Fourteen Points, which was the formation of the Covenant of the League of Nations. The goal of this organization was to encourage international cooperation to achieve international peace and security. One main point of the agreement was *Article X*. This stated that any war or threat of war to any of the members of the league would concern the whole league. The league would take any action that it thought necessary to safeguard the peace of nations. This included declaring war.

Reactions to the Treaty of Versailles

President Wilson's Fourteen Points had been very popular in Europe, especially among Germans. The Treaty of Versailles largely ignored them. France and Britain instead sought revenge and rewards. French Premier Clemenceau sarcastically dismissed the Fourteen Points, saying, "God only needed ten."

WOODROW WILSON (1856-1924)

Woodrow Wilson began his career as a professor of history and politics. He became president of Princeton University. Eight years later, he was elected governor of New Jersey. His writing and oratory attracted Democrats looking for a national leader. He was elected president in 1912. When the U.S. Senate refused to ratify the Treaty of Versailles, Wilson appealed directly to the public. Crowds cheered him as he toured the country. However, fragile health halted his tour. He lived until 1924 but never fully regained his mental or physical abilities.

The Germans resented the harsh settlement for years. It kept their economy weak. Their government was blamed for its inability to negotiate a more just and equal agreement.

Allied Reactions to the Treaty The Allies disagreed among themselves about the treaty. The British were generally happy. The French thought the terms did not punish Germany enough. Many Americans believed the terms too harsh. The Allied nations blamed one another for the problems they saw. And by admitting that there were problems, the Allies had difficulty standing up to Germany later on. They were unable to take a firm stand when Germany became aggressive again leading up to World War II.

U.S. Reaction to the Treaty When President Wilson returned after Versailles, he was unhappy that his Fourteen Points had been ignored. Moreover, the American public opposed the treaty he had just signed. In particular, Americans opposed the fact that the League of Nations could declare war for its member nations. The U.S. Constitution did not allow this. Many Americans did not want their government to give up authority to an outside power.

President Wilson launched a nationwide speaking tour in the summer of 1919. He hoped to gain support for the League of Nations. However, he suffered a serious stroke that ended both the tour and his attempts to gain support. Wilson's successor, President Warren G. Harding, later opposed the League of Nations.

WHAT DO YOU THINK?
Why did the American people oppose the Treaty of Versailles?

BELOW: *The peace treaty was signed in the Hall of Mirrors in the palace at Versailles, France.*

Other Treaties Based on Versailles

After the Treaty of Versailles, the Allies signed separate treaties with Austria, Bulgaria, Hungary, and the Ottoman Empire. On July 21, 1921, the U.S. Congress passed the Knox–Porter Resolution. This brought a formal end to the conflict between the United States and the Central Powers.

The Treaty of Saint-Germain-en-Laye
This treaty was signed on September 10, 1919, by the Allies and Austria. It dissolved the once-powerful Austro-Hungarian Empire. Many people who had been ruled by Austria-Hungary gained their independence. The treaty limited the Austrian army to 30,000 volunteers.

The Treaty of Neuilly-sur-Seine
Bulgaria and the Allies signed this treaty on November 27, 1919. It gave Bulgarian territories to Greece and the future Yugoslavia and limited the Bulgarian army to 20,000 men.

The Treaty of Trianon The Treaty of Trianon was signed on June 4, 1920, by the Allies and the Kingdom of Hungary. The Kingdom of Hungary was born when Austria-Hungary was dissolved. The treaty redefined its borders, with the new state making up only 28.6 percent of pre-war Hungary. Almost a third of Hungarians now lived outside of its borders. Hungary's army was limited to 35,000. The new kingdom had no direct access to the sea. This left it without a navy.

The Treaty of Lausanne After failing to sign the Treaty of Sèvres in 1920, Turkey signed the Treaty of Lausanne with the Allies on July 24, 1923. The treaty defined the borders of the modern Turkish state. Turkey gave up the Ottoman Empire, and the Allies recognized Turkey's new borders.

LEFT: *Mehmed VI, the last sultan of the Ottoman Empire*

CHAPTER 2

TECHNOLOGICAL ADVANCES

At the start of the war, newly discovered weapons, artillery, planes, and other military technologies did not fit with older military strategies. By the end of 1917, the major armies had modernized. The military benefited greatly from the global trend toward **industrialization** leading up to the war.

NEW AND IMPROVED WEAPONS

World War I changed warfare forever. New and more deadly weapons appeared. With World War I came machine guns, poison gas, and **aerial bombardments**. At the start of the war, carrier pigeons were used to send messages. By the end, early versions of sonar had been developed.

BELOW: *No Man's Land, Flanders Field, France*

Trench Warfare

Trench warfare was not new, but it was not widespread before World War I. When attacking troops encountered strong resistance, they would halt their attack and dig foxholes in the ground. Over time, they would connect these holes. This created long systems of trenches. Networks of trenches led back behind the front line so that supplies could be brought up from the rear.

The front trenches between two opposing armies were often 200 to 300 yards (183 to 274 m) apart. The space between the trenches was known as "No Man's Land."

The Weapons of Trench Warfare

The nature of trench warfare resulted in the development of many new weapons and new uses for old ones.

NO MANS LAND FLANDERS FIELD FRANCE 1919.

Barbed wire was first used in the U.S. by cattle ranchers. In World War I, it was used to protect trenches and slow enemy advances. Grenades and trench **mortars** could be used effectively against enemy soldiers at shorter ranges.

Advances in Weapons

Fierce and drawn-out fighting required stronger weapons both in and out of trenches. Machine guns were one of the war's most **lethal** developments. Capable of firing hundreds of rounds a minute, machine guns made crossing open ground deadly.

Infantry rifles, like the Lee Enfield Rifle, were developed that could fire faster and hold more bullets at once. Tracer bullets allowed a shooter to see the path of the bullet as it flew through the air. Early models of flamethrowers were also developed during the war.

Artillery caused the war's largest number of casualties. The use of artillery drastically changed during the war. In 1914, cannons were fired directly at their targets. By 1917, **indirect** fire from guns and mortars was much more common.

Germany was far ahead of the Allies in using heavy indirect fire. The Germans employed 6-inch (152 mm) and 12-inch (305 mm) howitzers. Typical French and British guns were only 3 inches (75 mm) and 4 inches (105 mm).

ABOVE: *Maxim machine gun*

Chemical Warfare

Both sides tried to break the trench war stalemate by any means possible. Deadly poison gas was one invention. Before the war ended, 50 types of chemical gas had been used. They caused long-term injury or painful death.

The Germans first used 4,500 cylinders of chlorine gas at Ypres in 1915. Phosgene gas, called the "choking gas," was 18 times more lethal than chlorine gas. Mustard gas turned out to be the most effective for both sides. The gas burned the skin, eyes, and lungs and caused painful blistering.

BELOW: *Gas masks provided some protection against poisonous gases used during the war.*

The Hague Conventions

The 1899 and 1907 Hague Conventions were treaties that outlawed the use of "poison or poisoned weapons." The Allies were outraged by the attacks. Still, they quickly developed their own versions of chemical warfare. As the war went on, both sides violated the terms of the Hague Conventions.

THE NEWEST LAND VEHICLE

Barbed wire, trenches, and bomb craters filled the World War I landscape. Both sides found crossing such terrain challenging. The British army developed a landship or "tank." This was a vehicle with a caterpillar tread. It could roll over trenches, flatten barbed wire, and provide cover for troops following behind it.

When 49 tanks first appeared in battle on September 15, 1916, in the Battle of the Somme, the Germans were terrified. Nothing seemed capable of stopping these strange, new vehicles. Within a year, the British were bringing hundreds of tanks to the battlefield.

In November 1917, at the Battle of Cambrai, tanks showed their potential. They did not need the usual preliminary bombardments for surprise attacks. The British tanks led an attack, breaking through the **Hindenburg Line**. Teams of British soldiers captured 8,000 enemy soldiers and drove back the German army 7 miles (11 km).

The mechanical reliability of the early tanks was questionable. Still, they soon became important weapons in the war. In fact, the French soon introduced a tank with a rotating turret, a dome-like structure on which weaponry could be mounted. The soldiers operating the weapons could turn the turret to aim at enemies on all sides.

The Germans used few of their own tanks. They focused on developing anti-tank guns and armor-piercing ammunition to fight the dreaded Allied tanks.

**WILFRED OWEN
(1893–1918)**

Wilfred Owen was an English soldier and a leading poet of World War I.

In 1917, Owen spent time recovering in a Scottish war hospital. He had a concussion and trench fever. There he met Siegfried Sassoon (an older English poet). Sassoon read his poems and offered him much encouragement. Owen was posted back to France in 1918. He was awarded the Military Cross for bravery. He was killed just one week before the armistice was signed. His poetry is known for its deep sense of compassion combined with grim realism.

ADVANCES IN AIRCRAFT

World War I saw the first large-scale use of aircraft. Technological advances allowed a military power to drop bombs on enemy soldiers from the air. Now, enemies could attack civilian populations. For the first time in history, all civilians in a country under attack risked their lives as much as soldiers did.

Airplanes

Airplanes were slowly introduced into the war effort on both sides. Early airplanes served mostly in observation, or scouting, work. As the war continued, planes got bigger, flew faster, traveled farther, and carried machine guns and bombs.

Pilots were glorified for their risky accomplishments in the air. An "ace" was a pilot who had shot down at least five enemy planes. Many young men wanted to become pilots because it was considered glamorous. Training was very tough, however, and the work was dangerous. Sixty percent of all pilot fatalities occurred during training. The average life expectancy of a British pilot who did survive training was only three to five weeks.

Observation Balloons and Zeppelins

Hydrogen-filled observation balloons anchored to the ground by a long rope were used early in the war for observing enemy troop movements. The Germans improved on this with the zeppelin. The zeppelin was a huge, cigar-shaped airship with engine-driven propellers. It had a gondola, or engine car, hanging below the balloon. Zeppelins could do bombing runs on places such as England and even Scotland. However, their hydrogen-filled balloons were highly flammable. The introduction of incendiary, or fire-starting, bullets made the zeppelins' "reign of terror" short-lived.

Advances in Aircraft Weaponry

Both sides needed ways to make their planes more efficient and to manufacture weapons to protect their aircraft and themselves. Eighteen pound (8 kg) anti-aircraft guns were developed, which could send artillery shells 2,000 yards (1,829 m) farther into the air. The introduction of interrupter gear on airplanes **synchronized** a machine gun mounted on a plane's nose with the rotation of the propeller. This allowed pilots to easily operate the guns by themselves. Bombers were developed, too, with larger fuel capacities, allowing them to travel farther and carry heavier loads. By the war's end, bombers could carry a bomb load as large as 1,750 pounds (794 kg).

ADVANCES IN NAVAL WARFARE

Before World War I, Britain had ruled the world's seas for hundreds of years. Its modernized shipbuilding industry and navy were the envy of other nations. Any country going up against the British navy would need a secret weapon to be successful.

ABOVE: *Zeppelins could be attacked and shot down during air battles.*

Naval Blockades

Soon after the war broke out, Britain began a naval blockade of Germany. Britain also set mines in international waters near Germany, which put neutral ships in danger. The blockade violated international law. Still, the blockade cut off vital military and civilian supplies. Germany created a blockade of its own. This blockade, however, was largely under the sea and featured newly improved submarines.

Submarines

At the beginning of the war, Britain had more submarines than Germany. To face the British navy, the Germans improved the design of their U-boats. They increased the boat's stability when traveling on the surface. U-boats became tougher and better equipped for long-distance travel. Germany dispatched them far into the North Sea to attack British ships.

Submarines proved their power on September 20, 1914, when a single U-boat sank three large British cruisers off the Dutch coast. This attack was the worst naval disaster the British navy had suffered in 300 years.

As the British naval blockade continued, Germany declared "unrestricted submarine warfare." This declaration meant that **U-boats** would target merchant ships as well as military ships. The goal was to stop supplies and starve Britain out of the war. German commanders ordered U-boats to attack any vessel traveling to or from Britain.

However, the plan might have backfired for Germany. On May 7, 1915, a U-boat sank the British liner RMS *Lusitania*, killing 1,198 people, including 128 Americans. Germany's unrestricted submarine warfare pushed America into the war on the side of the Allies.

Dreadnoughts

Just before the war began, the British had produced a new class of warship. The HMS *Dreadnought* was bigger and faster than any other ship. It had more guns and thicker armor. It was the first oil-powered fighting ship. All previous ships had been powered by coal. Germany built its own dreadnought-class ships.

BELOW: *The* Llandovery Castle, *a Canadian hospital ship, was sunk without warning by a German U-boat.*

Hydrophones (Pre-Sonar) and Depth Charges

With U-boats everywhere, Allied naval commanders wondered how to fight an enemy they could not see. American weapons experts developed the hydrophone, which could detect engine noise from enemy submarines underwater. This invention helped the Allies find a submarine and drop depth charges. Depth charges were bombs that were preset to explode at a certain depth. If a depth charge exploded even near a U-boat, it could damage or destroy the thin metal hull of the submarine.

BELOW *The British dreadnought* HMS Warspite *saw action in the Battle of Jutland in May 1916.*

OTHER TECHNOLOGICAL ADVANCES

Many other technologies were born out of the war. Two-way radio became important for communications. Searchlights helped ships navigate at night and spot incoming enemy aircraft. Electricity made a huge impact on World War I. Battleships could use electric systems to operate certain controls remotely or automatically.

WHAT DO YOU THINK?
Why did Germany risk U.S. entry into war by continuing to wage unrestricted submarine warfare?

MEDICAL ADVANCES

The Allied nations greatly expanded their medical services during the war. When the United States entered the war in 1917, the army did not yet have an established medical corps. The U.S. Army Medical Corps copied parts of the system that the French and British had been using for three years.

Wounds, Diseases, and Medical Practices

During World War I, doctors developed new ways to treat tissue damage, burns, and contagious diseases. Doctors learned that wounded soldiers had to be brought to the operating table within 12 hours. After that, the risk of infection greatly increased. Medics learned to clean wounds quickly and thoroughly. They used salt water to kill germs. That step was important because no medication could stop infection after it had started. Major improvements in **sanitation** and cleanliness decreased disease and the spread of infections.

A new system called **triage** helped doctors organize their responses, allowing doctors to care for more people. The tetanus vaccine was developed over the course of the war and perfected in 1924.

ABOVE: *The Red Cross provided help for wounded soldiers.*

Doctors began working on a typhoid vaccine during the war as well. Surgical advances, such as blood-typing, blood transfusions, use of **anesthetics** such as chloroform, and reconstructive surgical techniques, helped doctors to save more lives and better care for the wounded.

Shell Shock Some injuries were not physical. A mental illness caused by the terrors of war and the horrible living conditions became known as "shell shock." Sufferers of shell shock could be hysterical, confused, and unable to obey orders. Earlier, shell-shocked soldiers had been seen as weak or cowardly. As the war continued, shell shock became recognized as a serious medical condition.

Mobile Labs and X-Rays

Ambulance transport provided the most efficient way to remove the wounded from the battlefield. Motorized vehicles were still relatively new. They proved to be a huge advantage over having to carry injured soldiers by hand. The speed and efficiency of motorized ambulances made it practical to set up mobile labs closer to the front lines.

ABOVE: *The dazed look in the soldier's eyes was a common symptom of shell shock.*

These were called Casualty Clearing Stations. These stations were staffed by surgeons, anesthetists, and nurses. Those with severe injuries could be transferred to base hospitals far behind the lines. **Mobile** x-ray equipment was extremely useful as well, helping make emergency surgeries quicker and more successful.

BELOW: *Mobile x-ray truck*

CHAPTER 3

ECONOMIC AND SOCIAL CHANGES

In the early years of World War I, many soldiers were volunteers. In the later years, more were conscripted, or forced by the government, to serve through the draft. Many suffered horrific experiences, which left them **traumatized**. The Allied Powers lost over five million men. More than four million were taken prisoner or went missing. Of those fortunate enough to return home, nearly 13 million had been injured. Those who had fought were referred to as the "Lost Generation."

> A generation of innocent young men, their heads full of high abstractions like Honor, Glory, and England, went off to war to make the world safe for democracy. They were slaughtered in stupid battles planned by stupid generals. Those who survived were shocked, disillusioned and embittered by their war experiences, and saw that their real enemies were not the Germans, but the old men at home who had lied to them.
>
> SAMUEL HYNES (*A WAR IMAGINED*, 1991, PIMLICO)

For years afterward, people mourned the loss of loved ones. These included not only the dead, but also the wounded who would never recover and the missing. Many soldiers returned with shell shock. Some veterans blamed their suffering on the individuals and governments who had sent them into battle.

Back at home, surviving veterans often found that they could discuss the war only among themselves. To find ways to get together, they formed veterans' associations, or legions.

ALLIED NATIONS' ECONOMIES AFTER WORLD WAR I

Before the war began, the U.S. economy had been in recession, or decline. However, the war brought about an economic boom, or growth period, when Europeans started to purchase U.S. goods. When America entered the war, the U.S. government increased spending. Production shifted from civilian to war goods. Overall, unemployment fell from 7.9 percent to 1.4 percent, as the number of manufacturing jobs increased. The United States began investing internationally. After the war, with

Britain weakened, New York emerged as one of the world's leading financial centers. Furthermore, the U.S. had loaned billions of dollars to European nations. The United States quickly became the world's strongest nation economically.

Post-War Britain

Before the war, Britain had been one of the world's wealthiest nations. The war had been very expensive. It left Britain with a lot of debt. Interest payments on this debt amounted to about 40 percent of all government spending.

The war also undermined the British Empire's position in the world. Other nations, including Japan and **Communist** Russia, began to compete with Britain for colonies and resources. Britain could not keep up the level of armaments it needed to protect its worldwide empire.

Other members of the empire were affected significantly as well. By war's end, the Canadian government had introduced new policies that eventually led to a welfare system that provided assistance to needy families. Britain leaned heavily on Australia for supplies. Ordinary, working Australians were hit hard by shortages. New Zealand experienced labor shortages when many of the country's workers went to war. It also took on a lot of debt during the war. These challenges created social discontent that would lead to political change in some places.

BELOW: *At the end of the war there was food shortages in Britain. Here, Londoners line up to buy meat.*

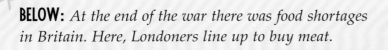

WHAT DO YOU THINK?
Why was the name "The Lost Generation" fitting for those who had fought in WWI?

ABOVE: *The Red Army captures the anti-Bolshevik White Army's artillery during the civil war in Russia.*

Post-War Russia

Invasion of its lands cut into Russia's ability to produce resources. Between that and the demands of supplying its army, Russia had no extra resources to sell to its allies. The Russian economy struggled along with the people. To finance the war, the government took out loans and printed money. This caused **inflation** to soar. By 1917, prices of goods had tripled in Moscow.

The civil war in Russia continued until 1921. Although the Bolsheviks took over the government, the rest of the world refused to recognize their leadership.

Other nations refused to trade with the new Russian government. Russia's economy suffered as a result.

THE GERMAN ECONOMY AFTER WORLD WAR I

Throughout the war, government **propaganda** led German citizens to believe they were winning. Only the military leaders knew that Germany was struggling on the battlefield. The British naval blockade kept food and goods from getting to Germany. German troops were poorly equipped. Most food went to the war effort, not to those at home.

Hyperinflation

The Treaty of Versailles dictated that Germany pay its war **reparations** in gold or foreign money only. With its gold spent, the German government bought foreign money with German marks, Germany's form of money. These purchases caused the value of the German mark to fall rapidly and the prices of German goods to rise. The German central bank then printed more money. This created **hyperinflation**, which meant that inflation could not be stopped. Many businesses went bankrupt, and unemployment became high. Germany ended up unable to pay its foreign debt as well.

As a result, workers were becoming even more unhappy. Many leaders feared that Germany might go the way of Russia and its "red revolution."

Stab-in-the-Back Legend

German leaders claimed that their armies had not really been defeated. In November 1918, when Germany surrendered, no Allied force had crossed into German lands. Leaders explained that Germany had to surrender because of the lack of support from home. This story became known as the stab-in-the-back legend. Its point was that Germany's defeat did *not* result from an inability to continue fighting. Instead, it resulted from the public's failure to respond to its "patriotic calling." Some politicians blamed the **republicans** who overthrew the monarchy. When Adolf Hitler came to power, his followers encouraged the idea that the Bolsheviks and the Jews had destroyed the German war effort on purpose.

ABOVE: *The German mark, the country's money, had become so worthless that it was used to light stoves.*

CHAPTER 4

POLITICAL SHIFTS

World War I resulted in many major political changes. Four major empires fell: the German, Russian, Austro-Hungarian, and Ottoman. The victorious Allied Powers would see significant changes as well.

ABOVE: *Posters pointed out the needs of working women.*

THE ROLE OF WOMEN

With large numbers of men going off to war, many jobs were left open. Women joined the workforce in numbers never seen before. On the home front during the war, women worked in factories and in the government. On the front lines, women served in the navy and marines. Thousands of women also volunteered as nurses.

In Britain before the war, about three million women worked outside the home. By January 1918, the number had reached five million. Women worked in shipbuilding and furnace stoking as well. Only men had held these jobs in the past.

When men returned from fighting, many women were forced out of jobs. Many wartime factories also closed. Women now found themselves struggling to find jobs. At this time, women were not considered equal to men in the workforce. Their job status was viewed as less important than men's.

Women and the Vote

Before World War I, American and British women did not have the right to vote. In the United States, the war provided a final push for women's **suffrage**. Protests and parades declared that 20 million women still did not have the same rights as men.

In Britain, the Representation of the People Act of 1918 granted women the right to vote on the same terms as men. In the United States, women's war work had increased support for women's suffrage. With the passage of the 19th Amendment in 1920, American women gained the right to vote.

ABOVE: *Suffragettes marched in many U.S. cities, including Boston.*

POLITICAL CHANGES IN RUSSIA

Even though Russia had withdrawn from the war, revolution continued there and in surrounding countries. People opposed to the Communist movement, called the Whites, fought the Bolsheviks' Red Army. By 1921, the Bolsheviks faced a trade **boycott**, exhaustion, starvation, and unrest within the Red Army itself.

The fighting dragged out. In time, it spread from Russia into neighboring countries. In 1922, through this series of revolutions, the United Soviet Socialist Republic (U.S.S.R.) was born.

POLITICAL CHANGES IN GREAT BRITAIN

War had left many British people with a growing distrust of political leaders and government officials. Many soldiers and civilians questioned why the war had been fought at all. They began to believe that government did not always serve their best interests.

Irish War of Independence

Ireland was once a free nation. It had been under British rule for hundreds of years. While fighting the Central Powers, Britain could not deal with Ireland's growing desire to be independent once again.

The Irish War of Independence began in January 1919. It started after the Irish Republic declared independence.

It was a conflict between British forces in Ireland and the Irish Republican Army. The pro-British Protestant majority fought the Irish nationalist Catholic minority in the northern provinces of Ireland. In July 1921, the war ended with the Anglo-Irish Treaty. This freed most of Ireland from British rule and established the Irish Free State.

In all of Ireland, six counties in the north remained loyal to Britain and became known as Northern Ireland. Violence would continue there for decades to come.

A Declining British Empire

World War I showed how much the British Empire depended on its self-governing **dominions**. Britain's control of many parts of its empire decreased after the war. Many British domains made important contributions to the war effort. This increased their standing within the empire. When Britain declared war in 1914, the members of the British Empire automatically were at war. At the end, Canada, Australia, and New Zealand all signed the Treaty of Versailles independently.

Canada World War I was the bloodiest conflict in Canada's history. More than 60,000 Canadians lost their lives. Canadian soldiers won recognition for their bravery, particularly on the battlefields of Ypres, Vimy Ridge, and Passchendaele. Canadian achievements became a source of national pride. Canada gained confidence that it could participate in global politics on its own strength.

RIGHT: *King George V (1865–1936) became Britain's king in 1910.*

Australia Australians made many contributions to the war, especially at Gallipoli. This helped the nation emerge as a member of the international community. Until the war, Britain had handled Australia's foreign affairs. However, as a World War I combatant, Australia sent its own representatives to the Paris Peace Conference in 1919. It also began to play a greater role politically in the Pacific region.

New Zealand In 1914, New Zealand's population was just over one million. World War I took more than 100,000 New Zealanders overseas. Being so far from home made them more aware of who they were and where they came from. It created a sense of a separate national identity. New Zealand soldiers referred to themselves as "kiwis."

Ultimately, the war took a heavy toll. New Zealand suffered almost 50 percent casualties among the 120,000 soldiers who enlisted. New Zealanders did not see a point to some battles. Some citizens did not support the fighting.

POLITICAL CLIMATE IN GERMANY

Even with the war over, conditions had not improved in Germany. In October 1918, Germany's naval command decided to confront the British navy in the hope of ending the blockade. To the sailors in the city of Kiel, such action seemed like certain death. Rather than go on the mission, the sailors **mutinied**. They killed some of their officers and took control of the ships. The incident sparked outrage in Germany. The Kiel sailors were seen as rebelling against high authority.

Other protests and demonstrations took place throughout the country. Those who had jobs went on strike, with soldiers joining the protests. By early November 1918, workers' and soldiers' councils had taken over a number of German cities. Politicians feared that Germany might experience a revolution like the one that happened in Russia.

Germany was in a dangerous political, social, and economic situation. The war had claimed over two million German soldiers. The country's industry could not recover without these men. They made up the core of Germany's workforce. Germany's economic problems seemed unavoidable.

The Beginning of the Weimar Republic

Germany desperately needed stronger leadership now that Kaiser Wilhelm no longer held power. The German people were upset that their economy was so poor. German politicians feared that the people would revolt against their government. In 1919, German delegates met in the city of Weimar to form a democratic government and write a constitution. The new government became known as the Weimar Republic, named for the city. Immediately, the new government faced serious problems. Germany was suffering from hyperinflation. The country had to obey the terms of the Treaty of Versailles.

RIGHT: *In 1919, Friedrich Ebert campaigned for the Social Democratic Party. He became the first president of the Weimar Republic.*

The new government also did not have strong support from German citizens.

Invasion of the Ruhr With hyperinflation and other economic problems, Germany could not meet its debt payments from the Treaty of Versailles. Germany's economic situation concerned France and Belgium, who were owed payments. In January 1923, French and Belgian troops occupied the German industrial region of the Ruhr Valley. They decided to take their payments in goods, such as coal from the Ruhr.

The German government asked Ruhr workers to use "passive resistance" against the invading troops. This plan had German coal miners and railway workers refusing to obey instructions given by the occupation forces. Production in the Ruhr came to a standstill. The measure was politically effective. But the consequences of passive resistance proved disastrous to the German economy.

It contributed further to hyperinflation and destroyed government **finances**. Wanting to reinvigorate Weimar's economy, the United States agreed to invest in Germany.

The Dawes Plan of 1924 The Dawes Plan of 1924 was created to help Germany out of hyperinflation and bring the economy some stability. The plan was named for the man who headed the committee, U.S. Vice President Charles Dawes. The nations on the Dawes Committee were the United States, Britain, Italy, Belgium, and France. The main points were simple: 1) control of the Ruhr was returned to Germany, 2) debt payments were **restructured** to make them easier to pay, and 3) Germany's national bank was restructured under Allied supervision. The U.S. was the world's most powerful nation. America's involvement with Weimar, Germany, reassured the rest of the world.

CHARLES GATES DAWES (1865–1951)

Vice President Charles Gates Dawes was known as "Uncle Sam's chief handyman." He had impressed many as a brigadier general supplying the U.S. Army in France during the war. After the war, he was the nation's first budget director. He saved $300 million in his first year.

Germany struggled to meet its enormous debt payments. Dawes helped come up with a plan to stabilize Germany's finances. The result was the Dawes Plan, for which he won the Nobel Peace Prize in 1925. After his term as U.S. Vice President ended in 1929, Dawes served as ambassador to Great Britain.

LEFT: *German money had lost so much value that it was used as a children's toy.*

35

The Young Plan Another plan was the Young Plan. On February 11, 1929, American Owen D. Young chaired a committee in Paris to create a new plan for Germany's recovery. This was a follow-up to the Dawes Plan. The Young Plan had three points. It reduced the amount of the debt payments due from Germany. It set up the Bank for International Settlements to handle the transfer of funds. It ended foreign controls on the German economy.

The Dawes and Young plans greatly increased America's economic ties to Europe. Unfortunately, the Young Plan was barely in effect when the **Great Depression** began. The Great Depression hit America and Europe especially hard. Germany's ability to repay its war debt quickly vanished completely.

Weimar's Golden Years

The years from 1924 through 1929 are known as the "Golden Age of Weimar." This period saw great improvement in Germany's stability, economic security, living standards, and cultural achievements.

Exceeding Expectations Many economists feared that the terms dictated by Versailles would hit German industry too hard. Germany had faced inflation, the occupation of Ruhr, and high unemployment. Still, the German economy began to see some improvements during the 1920s.

Germany had introduced a new currency, the *Rentenmark*, whose value was fixed to gold prices. The government asked for international assistance with its debt. The Dawes Plan was implemented. The German economy received more than 44 billion marks worth of foreign investment. More than half came from American loans. The rest was organized mostly through American bankers. Foreign money provided the resources needed for building new factories and upgrading old ones. Many factories used newly developed mechanization and assembly-line techniques.

By 1929, the German economy was beginning to stabilize and grow. Economic recovery introduced social reforms and better standards of living. Government programs were created to support the young, aged, unemployed, and disadvantaged.

The Middle Class Left Out Germany's economic recovery did not benefit everyone. The *Mittelschicht* (German for "middle class") found little to celebrate. The middle class was particularly hurt by hyperinflation. They did not benefit as much from new government policies. They also did not benefit from rising industrial wages. While unemployment had fallen for working-class jobs, it remained high for the middle class.

The Nazi Party

Even before the economic struggles of the 1920s, new political groups were emerging; 1919 saw the beginnings of the Nazi Party. It was called the German Workers' Party at this time. The group promoted German pride, **anti-Semitism**, and outrage at the terms of the Treaty of Versailles. Adolf Hitler joined the party the year it was founded. In July 1921, he assumed leadership of the organization. It was renamed the National Socialist German Workers' (Nazi) Party. It spoke loudly about injustices and the failures of the Weimar government. It held little influence until the Great Depression of the 1930s, when it gained great momentum and power.

ABOVE: *This cartoon shows Germany crushed by the terms of the Treaty of Versailles.*

Adolf Hitler

Before the Nazi Party began, Adolf Hitler served in the German army during World War I. In his climb to political power, Hitler used his speechmaking abilities to stir up Germans. Hitler declared that until a total revolution took place in German life, unemployment, hunger, and economic problems would continue.

Many Germans liked Hitler's ideas. He claimed that Germany deserved to regain the lands it had lost in the war. Hitler wanted to return Germany to its former place in world affairs. This meant freeing Germany from the economic and military restrictions it had suffered under since the Treaty of Versailles. Expansion of German land was also a key part of Hitler's policy. Hitler knew this would lead to war. Hitler's message fit with German nationalism. He also provided a group to blame for Germany's struggles, namely the Jews.

"November Criminals" Hitler directed much of his anger at the democratic parties in the *Reichstag*, or German parliament. He called them the "November criminals." He claimed that they had betrayed Germany by accepting the humiliating terms of the Treaty of Versailles. Hitler often used the stab-in-the-back legend to encourage anger and dissatisfaction in Germans.

ADOLF HITLER
(1889–1945)

Adolf Hitler was born on April 20, 1889, in Braunauam Inn, Austria. His father was short-tempered, strict, and often brutal. His mother took Hitler's side when his father lashed out against him. In 1905, he dropped out of school, and moved to Vienna. He hoped to become an artist. He applied twice to the Academy of Fine Arts but was rejected both times. During this period, he began to develop his hatred of the Jews.

In 1914, Hitler joined the German army. He was not popular with his comrades. Still, he was awarded six medals, including the Iron Cross. A month before the end of the war, Hitler was temporarily blinded by a gas attack. While he was recovering, Germany surrendered. Hitler was devastated. Like many other Germans, Hitler felt that Germany had been betrayed by its leaders. He thought the terms of the Treaty of Versailles were humiliating.

The End of the Weimar Republic

In spite of prosperity during the 1920s, the end of the decade saw the world caught in the midst of the Great Depression. By 1931, the German government faced bankruptcy. Public employees were taking huge pay cuts. Taxes had been drastically increased. The economy had slumped, and unemployment rates had shot up. Riots broke out in the streets. Banks collapsed, and foreigners pulled their money and investments out of the country.

Germany's biggest problem was its foreign debt, which had to be paid in U.S. dollars. Credit flowing into Germany came to a halt. Withdrawals of U.S. dollars from German banks quickly drained Germany's cash reserves.

The government tried cutting government spending by almost a third, raised taxes, and cut wages. However, a year later, unemployment had increased to 30 percent. Money was still pouring out of the country.

To help Germany, U.S. President Herbert Hoover proposed a one-year halt on Germany's foreign debt. By the time Congress finally approved the proposal, it was too late. In the summer of 1931, German banks failed and closed. The German government failed to pay its debts.

THE GREAT DEPRESSION

This collapse of the German economy came in the midst of the global economic downturn known as the Great Depression. By 1928, Germany, Brazil, and the countries of Southeast Asia were all economically depressed. By early 1929, the economies of Poland, Argentina, and Canada were feeling the impact. The U.S. economy followed in the middle of 1929. Many countries were deep in debt after the war. Their governments dealt with this by printing more money. This caused the prices of goods to rise. With unemployment high, people could not afford to buy as much. Governments struggled to find ways to get their economies out of the rut.

BELOW: *During the Depression, hungry and unemployed New Yorkers stood in lines for free food.*

ABOVE: *Hitler at a 1925 Nazi Party meeting*

> First they came for the communists, and I didn't speak out because I wasn't a communist. Then they came for the trade unionists, and I didn't speak out because I wasn't a trade unionist. Then they came for the Jews, and I didn't speak out because I wasn't a Jew. Then they came for me, and there was no one left to speak out for me.
>
> MARTIN NIEMÖLLER
> 1892–1984

The Rise of the Nazi Party

The Great Depression and the collapse of Germany's economy provided an opportunity for Hitler and the emerging Nazi Party. Through the 1920s, Hitler had been speaking about the problems of unemployment, inflation, hunger, and economic issues. His speeches attracted new people to the party. Many young, economically disadvantaged Germans joined the Nazis.

In 1923, in Munich, Hitler and his followers staged the "Beer Hall *Putsch*," an attempted takeover of the government in the German state of Bavaria. Hitler had hoped this would spark a larger revolution against the national government. Instead, Hitler and others were arrested. Hitler received a five-year prison sentence, although he actually served less than a year. While in prison, he wrote the first volume of his political autobiography, *Mein Kampf* (German for *My Struggle*).

The Beer Hall *Putsch* and Hitler's trial received much attention from the press. The attention turned him into a national figure in Germany. When he was released from prison, Hitler began rebuilding the Nazi Party through the electoral process.

The Nazi Party won the greatest share of the popular vote in the two *Reichstag* general elections of 1932. Hitler created a political alliance between the National Socialist German Workers' Party, or NSDAP, and the German National People's Party.

Finally, in 1933, Hitler became **chancellor** of Germany. In the following months, he rapidly brought all aspects of German life under the control of his party. By June 1933, few organizations remained outside state control, aside from the army and churches.

Nazi Party Ideologies Nazism had several core ideals. *Authoritarianism* said that the Nazi Party was led and controlled by one single person. *Totalitarianism* meant that government control extended into German political, social, and cultural life. *Nationalism* supported Germany's economic self-sufficiency and encouraged loyalty to the German people first. *Militarism* said that Germany's military needed to be rearmed. *Expansionism* proposed that all people of the German race should be combined into a greater German state. *Racialism* said that blonde-haired and blue-eyed Germans were better than other races. Jews, Slavs, and Roma were seen as racially inferior.

The Hitler Youth The Hitler Youth movement grew out of Hitler's belief that the future of Nazi Germany was its children. Created in the 1920s, the Hitler Youth had 100,000 members in 1933. After Hitler came to power, he outlawed all other youth movements. By 1936, Hitler Youth membership had grown to four million.

Hitler Youth catered to 10- to 18-year-old boys and girls. Boys trained for military service. Girls prepared for motherhood. Boys engaged in "military athletics," such as bayonet drill, grenade throwing, gas defense, and pistol shooting. Girls had to run 66 yards (60 meters), throw a ball, swim 109 yards (100 meters), and know how to make a bed.

Teachers complained that students were so tired from attending evening meetings of the Hitler Youth that they could barely stay awake the next day at school. By 1938, attendance at Hitler Youth meetings had fallen to barely 25 percent. The authorities made attendance required.

WHAT DO YOU THINK?

To the outside world, the Hitler Youth appeared to personify German discipline. How do we know that not everyone liked the movement?

ABOVE: *Hitler Youth rally in Nuremberg, 1933*

Hitler's Neighborly Relations

Hitler's dream was to recapture German lands. He made this promise to his followers. He began making moves toward this goal in 1936.

The Rhineland On March 7, 1936, Hitler sent German troops into the demilitarized zone in the Rhineland. That violated the Treaty of Versailles. Around the world, people protested the move. No nations, however, took action against it.

Austria In February 1938, Hitler informed Austrian Chancellor Kurt von Schuschnigg that Germany needed to secure its frontiers. Schuschnigg tried to call a vote on maintaining Austrian independence. Hitler demanded that

the vote be cancelled. German armed forces entered Austria the next day. Schuschnigg resigned that evening.

Czechoslovakia The Sudetenland, in the newly created country of Czechoslovakia, was home to a substantial number of Germans. Hitler believed that because many Germans lived there, the Sudetenland should be part of Germany. Under pressure from separatist groups within the Sudeten German Party, the Czech government offered economic benefits to the region. British Prime Minister Neville Chamberlain arranged a series of meetings with Hitler. Chamberlain hoped to avoid war. These talks resulted in the Munich Agreement, signed on September 30, 1938.

German Expansion Prior to World War II

0 — 200 miles
0 — 200 km

Sweden

Latvia

NORTH SEA

Denmark

Annexation
of Memel
March 1939

BALTIC SEA

Lithuania

Great Britain

Danzig

East Prussia

Netherlands

Berlin

Warsaw

Belgium

Germany

Claiming the Sudetenland
September 1938 and
Czechoslovakia March 1939

Poland

Reunification with Saar
region January 1935
and Reoccupation of
Rhineland March 1936

Prague

Luxembourg

France

Munich

Czechoslovakia

Vienna

Annexation
of Austria
March 1938

Switzerland

Austria

Hungary

Italy

Romania

Yugoslavia

‖ Regions of German expansion
1936–1939

The agreement forced the Czechoslovak government to accept the German annexation of the Sudetenland. The agreement lasted for six months, until Hitler seized the rest of Czechoslovakia.

Invasion of Poland and the Beginning of World War II

Hitler became bolder after these successes. He demanded the return of the Free City of Danzig and the Polish Corridor in 1939. This corridor was a strip of land that separated German East Prussia from the rest of Germany. Britain said it would come to the aid of Poland if it was attacked. Hitler thought the British were bluffing. Germany invaded Poland on September 1, 1939. Britain and France declared war on Germany two days later. World War II was underway.

LEGACIES OF WORLD WAR I

American involvement in World War I and President Wilson's administration became deeply unpopular. In the period between the wars, Congress passed laws to keep the U.S. neutral in future conflicts. World War I had left millions dead, permanently disabled, and mentally damaged. However, the legacy of the Great War goes beyond its effects in the United States.

ABOVE: *World War I Memorial, Kansas City, Missouri*

Four large and powerful empires fell, never to be resurrected. Furthermore, historians connect World War I with the most influential events of the 20th century: the Bolshevik Revolution in Russia, World War II, the Holocaust, and the development of the atomic bomb. Others trace connections, even if indirect, to the Great Depression, the Cold War, and the collapse of European **colonialism**. World War I also contributed to the rise of fascism in Italy. It triggered colonial revolts in the Middle East and in Southeast Asia. By weakening or destroying European economies, the war left the United States as the world's leading power. Even the modern political situation of the Middle East, including the Arab–Israeli conflict, has its roots in the splitting up of the Ottoman Empire at the end of World War I.

Lessons from Versailles

The Treaty of Versailles demonstrated the danger of allowing vengeance to play a leading role in foreign affairs.

After World War I, many thought the Versailles treaty had been too harsh. Germany had been treated as though it were the only cause of the war. The terms of the treaty were harsh enough to fuel the rage of the German people for decades to come. World leaders would remember this as they tried to construct a peace at the end of World War II.

WHAT DO YOU THINK?
How do you think world leaders would apply the lessons of the Treaty of Versailles at the end of World War II?

FURTHER READING AND WEBSITES

BOOKS

Berg, A. Scott. *Wilson*. New York: Putnam, 2013.

Best, Nicholas. *The Greatest Day in History: How, on the Eleventh Hour of the Eleventh Day of the Eleventh Month, the First World War Finally Came to an End.* Philadelphia: PublicAffairs, 2008.

Freedman, Russell. *The War to End All Wars: World War I.* New York: Clarion Books, 2010.

Hollihan, Kerrie Logan. *Rightfully Ours: How Women Won the Vote.* Chicago: Review Press, 2012.

Mackersey, Ian. *No Empty Chairs: The Short and Heroic Lives of the Young Aviators Who Fought and Died in the First World War.* London: Weidenfeld & Nicolson, 2012.

Macmillan, Margaret. *Paris 1919: Six Months That Changed the World.* New York: The Random House Publishing Group, 2003.

Remarque, Erich Maria and A. W. Wheen. *All Quiet on the Western Front.* New York: Fawcett Books, 1987.

Weitz, Eric D. *Weimar Germany: Promise and Tragedy.* Princeton: Princeton University Press, 2009.

Shirer, William L. *The Rise and Fall of the Third Reich: A History of Nazi Germany.* New York: Simon and Schuster, 1987.

WEBSITES

Then & Now: The Shaping of the 21st Century
www.pbs.org/greatwar/ thenandnow/index.html

Rise of Nazism
www.museumofworldwarii.com rise-of-nazism

World War I Related Records: Records of the American Commission to Negotiate Peace
www.archives.gov/research/ foreign-policy/related-records/ rg-256.html

GLOSSARY

abdicate	to formally give up power; surrender a throne
aerial bombardments	continuous firing of artillery from airplanes
alliance	formal association of nations or groups
anesthetics	a substance that causes a patient to not feel pain
annexed	incorporated territory into a larger existing political unit
anti-Semitism	anti-Jewish beliefs; hostility toward the Jewish population
armistice	an agreement to stop fighting a war
Baltic States	countries within Europe's eastern peninsulas, modern-day Slovenia, Croatia, Bosnia and Herzegovina, Serbia, Kosovo, Montenegro, Macedonia, Albania, Bulgaria, Romania, and Moldova
blockade	isolation or blocking a harbor to stop people or supplies from entering or leaving the country
boycott	refusing to buy from or deal with a person, nation, or business
ceasefire	a military order to stop fighting
chancellor	chief minister or head of state
cholera	a disease that causes severe vomiting and diarrhea and can cause death
colonialism	policies through which a nation maintains control over dependent, foreign territories
combatants	people or nations that fight or participate in battles or a war
Communist	relating to an economic system based on the idea that wealth and property would be owned by the community as a whole
counterattacks	attacks by a defending force against an attacking enemy force to regain lost ground
culture	the controlled growing of microorganisms
czar	a Russian king; one of the former emperors of Russia
demilitarized	prohibited from having military forces or installations
dominated	ruled over or controlled; stood out above all others
dominions	the smaller countries that make up an empire
exiled	forced to leave his or her home or country
fascism	a government with a dictator who controls the economy and will not tolerate opposition

finances	management of money, banking, credit, and investments
Great Depression	the most severe economic downturn in recent history; began in 1929, lasted into the 1930s
Hindenburg Line	a German defensive position on the Western Front
hyperinflation	when money loses its value very quickly, causing the prices of goods and services to increase substantially
indirect	not in a direct path; scattered
industrialization	building factories to improve manufacturing output
inflation	when money loses its value, causing prices to increase
lethal	deadly; highly destructive
Marxist	according to the ideas of Karl Marx; belief in a classless society where workers would control the means of production
mobile	easily movable
mobilized	assembled and prepared for war
mortars	short-barreled cannons that can send explosives high into the air
mutinied	revolted against their commanding officer
nationalism	devotion to the interests or culture of a particular nation
neutral	not aligned with or supporting a side in a war or dispute
oratory	skill in public speaking
propaganda	ideas, information, or rumors spread for the purpose of helping or hurting an organization, issue, or person
reparations	money or payments owed by a country or group that loses a war
republicans	people who favor government in which officials are elected
restructured	organized or arranged in a different way
sanitation	using measures, such as cleanliness and disposal of trash and human waste, to protect public health
stalemate	a situation in which further action is blocked; a deadlock
suffrage	the right to vote
synchronized	caused two or more things to happen at the same time
traumatized	experienced horrible things that resulted in emotionally injuries
triage	sorting injured people into groups depending on the seriousness of their injuries
typhoid	an infectious disease that often leads to death from high fever, delirium, and an intense rash
U-boats	German submarines; short for *Unterseebooten*
ultimatum	statement of terms that expresses or implies the threat of serious penalties if the terms are not met

INDEX